P·I·C·T·U·R·E·P·E·D·I·A

NOTE TO PARENTS

This book is part of PICTUREPEDIA, a completely
new kind of information series for children.
Its unique combination of pictures and words
encourages children to use their eyes to discover and
explore the world, while introducing them to a wealth
of basic knowledge. Clear, straightforward text
explains each picture thoroughly and provides
additional information about the topic.

'Looking it up' becomes an easy task with
PICTUREPEDIA, an ideal first reference for all types of
schoolwork. Because PICTUREPEDIA is also entertaining,
children will enjoy reading its words and looking
at its pictures over and over again. You can encourage
and stimulate further inquiry by helping your child
pose simple questions for the whole family to
'look up' and answer together.

ENERGY AND INDUSTRY

A DORLING KINDERSLEY BOOK
Conceived, edited and designed by DK Direct Limited

Consultant Roger Bridgman

Project Editor Sarah Miller

Art Editor Liz Black
Designer Samantha Webb

Series Editor Sarah Phillips
Series Art Editor Ruth Shane

Picture Researcher Miriam Sharland

Production Manager Ian Paton

Editorial Director Jonathan Reed
Design Director Ed Day

First published in Great Britain in 1994
by Dorling Kindersley Limited
9 Henrietta Street
London WC2E 8PS

Reprinted 1997

A CIP catalogue record for this book
is available from the British Library.

ISBN 0-7513-5120-2

Reproduced by Colourscan, Singapore
Printed and bound in Italy by Graphicom

ENERGY AND INDUSTRY

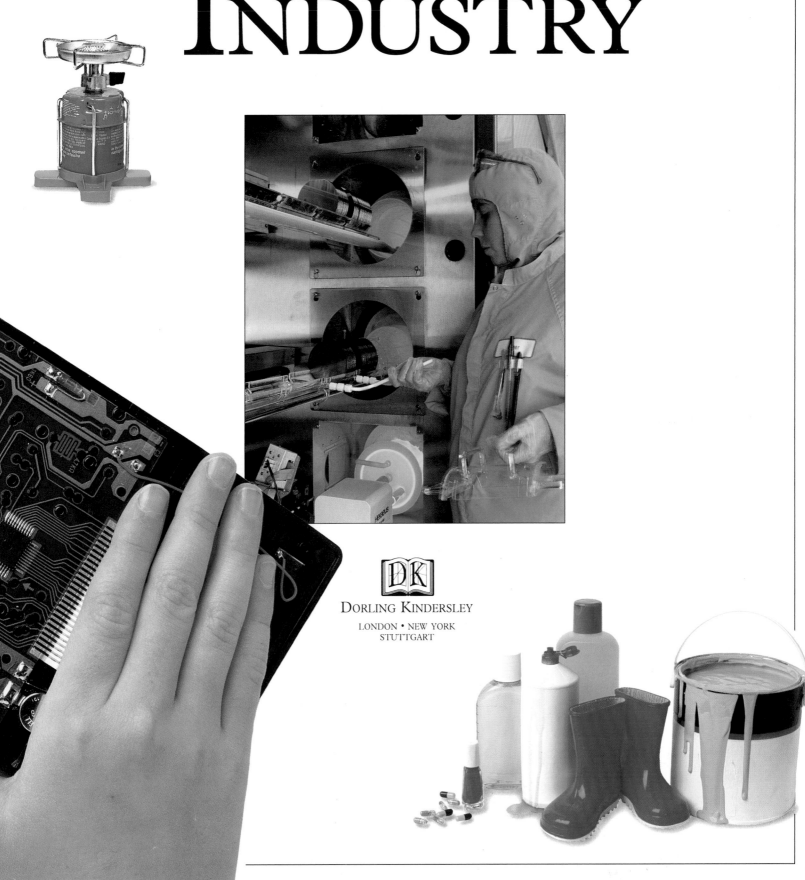

DK
DORLING KINDERSLEY
LONDON • NEW YORK
STUTTGART

CONTENTS

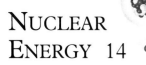

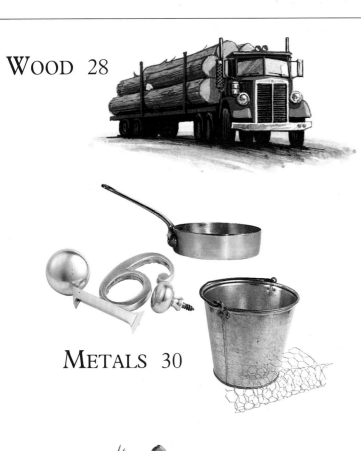

ENERGY

Nothing can happen without energy. It makes plants grow, machines move and lights shine. Almost all this energy comes from a giant nuclear furnace called the Sun. The energy from sunlight that fell to Earth millions of years ago is now stored in the ground in the form of coal, oil or natural gas. These fossil fuels are being burnt 1,000 times faster than they are being made, so one day there may be none left to power factories or your home.

Burning Out
Heat and light energy are released when a fuel is burnt. The light from a candle comes from the energy stored in the wax.

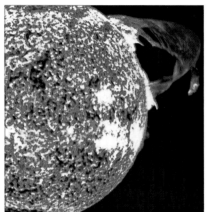

Surface of the Sun

Stored Sunlight
Fossil fuels are the cheapest and easiest source of energy. They still supply about 90 per cent of the world's needs.

About one-third of the energy used in the world comes from coal.

Coal could last for at least 200 more years.

Fountain of Fire
An enormous amount of energy is trapped inside the Earth. You can see this when a volcano shoots out lava. Scientists are trying to tap into this unused energy to solve the energy shortage.

More oil is used than any other fuel, but it may run out in about 40 years.

The energy in one gram of oil could run a television for nearly four minutes.

The energy in one gram of coal could run a television for about two minutes.

Stop the Rot

The coal that is used today comes from plants that grew in swamps about 300 million years ago. Energy from the Sun is trapped inside the plants because they were buried before they could rot away.

A layer of plants five times taller than you is squashed into a band of coal which is about as wide as the distance between your elbow and your wrist.

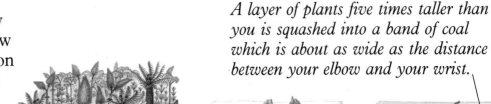

Long before dinosaurs lived, swampy forests covered much of the Earth.

1. Trees and giant ferns died, fell over and began to rot.

2. Masses of mud covered the plants and squashed them into coal.

3. The super-squashed band of coal is now buried deep underground.

The energy in wind, waves and waterfalls will last for millions of years. But at the moment, it only supplies a tiny part of the energy the world uses.

You can save energy by remembering to switch off lights when they are not needed.

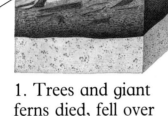

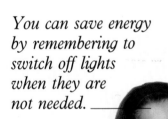

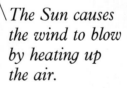

Spark of Energy

Industry is one of the biggest users of energy. For example, an enormous amount is needed to melt scrap metal to make steel in an electric arc furnace. The energy needed to make just one kilogram of steel could run a small car for a whole hour.

The Sun causes the wind to blow by heating up the air.

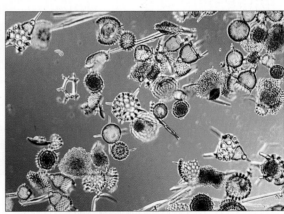

Small Start

Tiny plants and animals float in the sea. Some of those that lived millions of years ago have been buried and squashed to form oil and natural gas.

There may be no natural gas left in about 60 years' time.

The energy in one gram of nuclear fuel could run a television for more than 80 days!

COAL

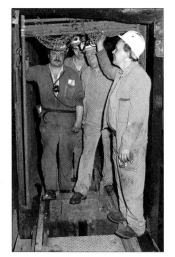

Like layers of cream in a cake, there are bands, or seams, of coal in the rocks beneath the ground. Some seams are near enough to the surface to be scraped out with diggers. This is called opencast mining. But most seams are found deeper down and have to be dug up by miners using massive machines. About half of the 5,000 million tonnes of coal mined each year is burnt in power stations to generate electricity.

Cooking Coke
Coal is put into giant ovens and baked at more than 900°C. When the oven door is opened, coke topples out. Coke is needed to make steel.

Coke is coal minus tar, oils and gases.

The tar that collects at the bottom of a coke oven is used to make soap!

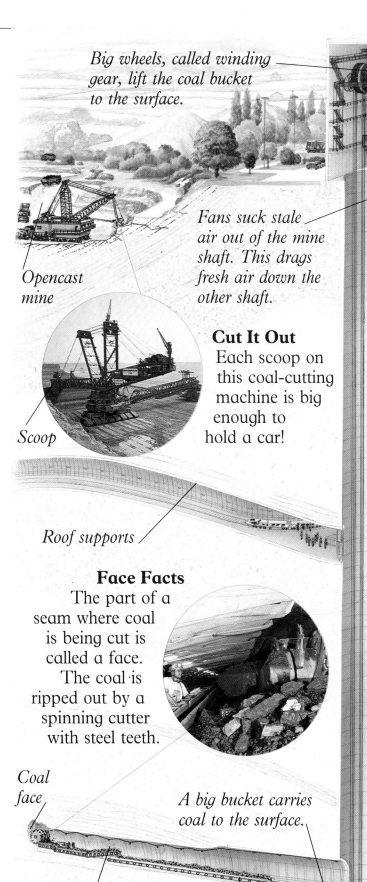

Big wheels, called winding gear, lift the coal bucket to the surface.

Opencast mine

Fans suck stale air out of the mine shaft. This drags fresh air down the other shaft.

Cut It Out
Each scoop on this coal-cutting machine is big enough to hold a car!

Scoop

Roof supports

Face Facts
The part of a seam where coal is being cut is called a face. The coal is ripped out by a spinning cutter with steel teeth.

Coal face

A big bucket carries coal to the surface.

Water is sprayed onto the coal to cut down the coal dust.

Conveyor belt

Pumps take water from the bottom of the mine.

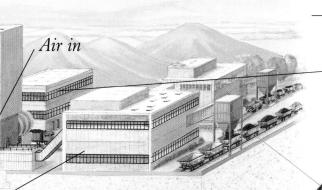

Air in

The coal is washed and separated into different-sized lumps before it leaves the mine.

Cages carry miners down a deep shaft.

The main shaft was blown out of the rock with explosives.

Long tunnels are dug to reach new coal seams.

Boring!
Big machines chew through the rock to open up new tunnels.

Mine shafts can be 1,200 metres deep.

Computer control room

Burning to Go
Nonstop trains take coal straight to the power station.

All Aboard!
Miners travel on trains to coal faces that are many kilometres away from the shaft.

Most of the coal in this seam has already been dug out.

A breeze can always be felt in the tunnel as the air moves through the mine.

Down to Earth
Not all coal is the same. Hard coals, which are found deeper underground, release more energy when they burn.

Half-squashed coal, or peat, is made into fuel bricks.

Soft, crumbly brown coal is burnt to make coke.

Black bituminous coal is burnt to generate electricity.

Anthracite coal is used in houses and factories.

Davy's safety lamp

Seeing the Light
Miners once worked by candlelight but the flames often set fire to the explosive gases that build up in tunnels. In 1815, a safety lamp was invented. Its flame was kept behind a wire mesh. Modern lamps are even safer as they are battery powered.

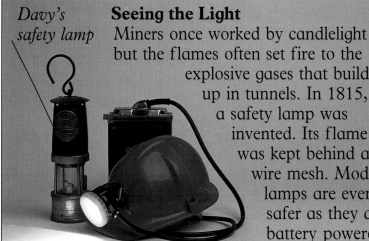

OIL

In the rocks under hot deserts, snowy plains and stormy seas there is buried treasure: a 'liquid gold' called oil. Most of this sticky, black fossil fuel is used for energy but twelve per cent of each barrel is turned into chemicals and plastics. All oil is brought to the surface by drilling deep holes called wells. On land this is fairly easy, but at sea platforms as tall as skyscrapers have to be built.

Sandstone

Sandstone with oil

Solid 'Sponge'
Oil is found in the tiny spaces in rocks such as sandstone. This oily layer is often sandwiched between water and a layer of natural gas.

Natural gas

Trapped oil

Water

Each marble stands for a grain of rock.

A Boring Bit
A sharp-toothed metal cutter, called a bit, bores through rock to reach oil. Drill bits are replaced twice a day as they wear out quickly.

During drilling, chemicals are pumped around the bit to carry rubble up to the surface.

This is a model of an oil platform, called Brent C, in the North Sea.

Unwanted gas is burnt from the top of a tall tower.

Two hundred people live and work on this oil platform.

Drilling pipes hang from a tower called a derrick.

Helicopter

Lifeboat

Every day, one quarter of a million barrels of hot, freshly drilled oil are pumped into the hollow concrete legs to cool down.

Some oil is piped into a gigantic, underwater storage tank.

Cooled oil is piped ashore.

Explosives are used to make cracks in the rock so that oil can flow into the wells.

Gas

An arched layer of oil-proof rock, such as granite, traps oil underneath it.

Oil

Water

Wells fan out to reach the oil.

Only Way Out
A 1,284-kilometre-long pipe snakes across the snowy wastes of Alaska. Oil takes a whole week to flow down the pipe to reach an ice-free port in the South.

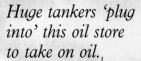

Oil at Sea
Huge structures, called rigs, drill down to find oil. At sea, some rigs float on the surface but others stand on the sea bed.

Huge tankers 'plug into' this oil store to take on oil.

Tankers can take oil all over the world.

Look how big this rig is compared to the Statue of Liberty!

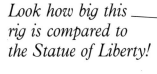

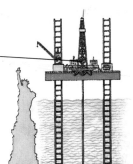

Jack-up rig

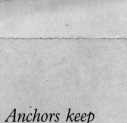

Anchors keep the oil store on the sea bed.

Pump It Up
Not all oil gushes to the surface naturally. Some is pumped up by machines called nodding donkeys! This 'donkey' has been painted to look like a grasshopper.

Drill ship

Semi-submersible rig

This zigzag break in the picture is to show that oil is usually found under thousands of metres of rock.

Gas gushes out when the pressure is released.

Wildcat Wanted?
Before a well is dug, geologists must be sure that the rocks below the ground are the right shape to trap oil. A test drill, or 'wildcat', is only started if the surveys and satellite pictures look good.

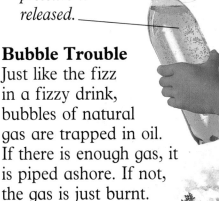

Bubble Trouble
Just like the fizz in a fizzy drink, bubbles of natural gas are trapped in oil. If there is enough gas, it is piped ashore. If not, the gas is just burnt.

NATURAL GAS

What a Whiff!
Natural gas
has no smell.
Chemicals are
added to it so
that leaks can
be smelt.

In 1918, a gas was discovered in an oilfield in Texas. It was named natural gas because it replaced a gas that was manufactured from coal. This new fuel is now used in factories and homes across the world. Natural gas travels a long way before it reaches the top of your stove, to burn as a bright blue flame. It has to be released from deep below the ground, cleaned, and piped countless kilometres.

The journey begins at a gas rig.

Mostly Methane
Natural gas contains three different gases. Butane and propane are taken out at a gas terminal. Methane, the part that burns best, is sent through pipes to houses and factories.

Butane gas camping stove

Gas terminal

Giant fans waft natural gas along the pipes.

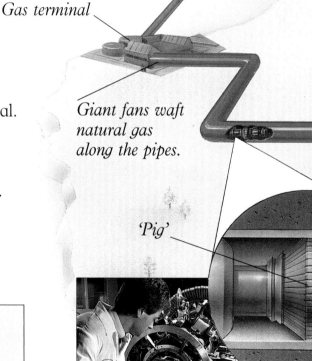

Pipe

'Pig'

Soil

Cool It
Ships take methane to places that are not connected to pipelines. The gas is cooled into a liquid so that it takes up 600 times less room.

If it is cooled into a liquid, a balloonful of methane gas can fit into a space the size of a pea.

Methane is cooled to -162°C to make it turn into a liquid.

Methane tank

Very Important Pig
'Pigs', not people, check natural gas pipes! A 'pig' is a computer on wheels that whizzes down pipes to pinpoint cracks and other problems.

On the Way Up

This big building, called a rig, gathers up gas that flows from deep under the sea bed. The drill to reach the pocket of gas may be six kilometres long.

Some gas is stored near homes to supply sudden daily demands – such as at dinner time!

The roof floats on top of the gas. So the lower the roof is, the less gas is left.

Iron pipe

Gas is sent through pipes to homes and factories.

The plastic gas pipe is dragged through the tunnel by the 'mole'.

Road

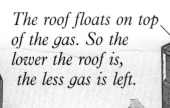

The 'mole' smashes through the earth like a pneumatic drill.

Pumping stations keep the gas moving.

'Mole' hole

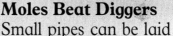

You could stand up in the pipe that travels between the rig and the terminal.

A dog could fit into the pipe that links factory pipes to gas-terminal pipes.

It is roomy enough for a cat to sit inside the pipes that take gas to factories.

A mouse could fit into the small plastic pipe that goes into your home.

Growing Gas

Farms off the coast of California grow a giant seaweed, called kelp. It is harvested three times a year by special ships and then put in tanks and left to rot. The decaying kelp gives off methane gas.

Moles Beat Diggers

Small pipes can be laid without digging up streets using a rocket-like machine, called a 'mole'. Its route is guided by a computer.

NUCLEAR ENERGY

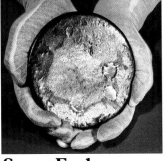

Super Fuel
One handful of pure uranium can release as much energy as 72,000 barrels of oil!

Not so Fast
This drawing shows very simply how neutrons whizz around a nuclear reactor and crash into uranium atoms in fuel rods.

Atoms are the tiny particles that make up the whole universe. Enormous amounts of energy are locked inside atoms. When billions of uranium atoms are torn apart in a nuclear power station the energy that is set free can boil water. Steam from this hot water is used to generate electricity. People worry about nuclear power because when the energy is released from an atom, deadly rays, called radiation, also escape.

2. The splitting uranium atoms inside the fuel rod 'shoot out' new neutrons which travel at 16,000 kilometres a second.

1. Energy is released when neutrons hit atoms in the fuel rods.

Water warms up

Fuel rod

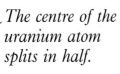

A neutron collides with an atom.

The centre of the uranium atom splits in half.

Energy and radiation

Two or three new neutrons escape. Each one can collide with another atom and set free more energy.

Cold water

Old fuel rods are radioactive 'rubbish'.

Fission Division
The heart of an atom, called a nucleus, is made up of neutrons and protons. These are held together by energy. When an atom is split, some of this energy is set free. Splitting an atom to release energy is called fission.

Cool It
Fuel rods are replaced every few years. Before the reusable uranium can be removed from them, the rods are cooled in a special pond.

Inside this building, a turning turbine generates electricity.

The nuclear reactor is in here.

A Powerful Building
The nuclear reactor is surrounded by thick concrete walls. These make sure that dangerous radiation does not escape.

The reactor is under this red steel floor.

Moderator

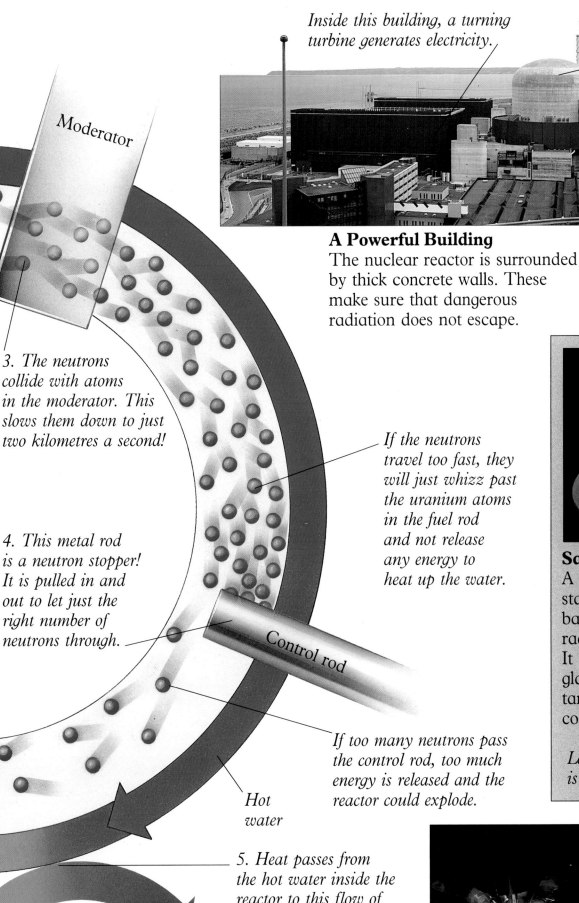

3. The neutrons collide with atoms in the moderator. This slows them down to just two kilometres a second!

If the neutrons travel too fast, they will just whizz past the uranium atoms in the fuel rod and not release any energy to heat up the water.

4. This metal rod is a neutron stopper! It is pulled in and out to let just the right number of neutrons through.

Control rod

If too many neutrons pass the control rod, too much energy is released and the reactor could explode.

Hot water

5. Heat passes from the hot water inside the reactor to this flow of cold water. The cold water boils into steam.

Laser beam

6. The powerful jet of steam turns a turbine to generate electricity.

Safe Deposit?
A typical nuclear power station produces about 20 bathfuls of very dangerous radioactive waste each year. It is made into a sort of glass and poured into steel tanks, which are coated in concrete and buried.

Less dangerous waste is buried in barrels.

Sunny Future
When super-hot atoms collide, they fuse together and set energy free. It is this fusion that makes the Sun shine. Scientists are trying to build 'Suns' on Earth by firing lasers at atoms.

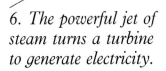

ENDLESS ENERGY

When oil, gas and coal run out, people will need other sources of energy to fuel their cars and light their houses. Wind and water are already being put to work but the best hope for an endless supply of free energy is the Sun. Light and heat from the Sun pour down onto the Earth all the time. Today, sunshine runs calculators, watches and even power stations. One day scientists hope to collect sunlight in space and beam it back to Earth!

What a Gas!
In some countries manure is collected, tipped into containers and left to rot. The gas it gives off is piped to homes and used for cooking and heating.

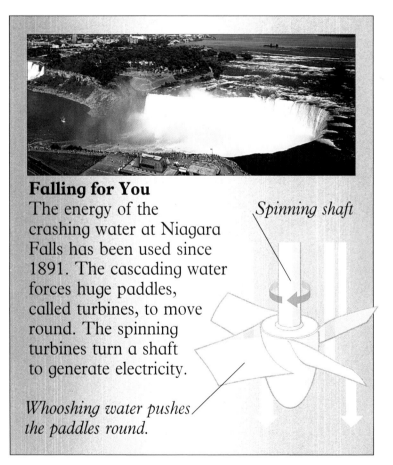

Falling for You
The energy of the crashing water at Niagara Falls has been used since 1891. The cascading water forces huge paddles, called turbines, to move round. The spinning turbines turn a shaft to generate electricity.

Spinning shaft

Whooshing water pushes the paddles round.

Trick of the Light
This is the world's first solar power station. It was built in 1969 at Odeillo in France. Electricity is generated by using reflected sunlight to boil water into steam.

This enormous mirror is curved so that all the sunshine that hits it is reflected onto one small spot at the top of the tower.

Computers keep the 63 mini-mirrors facing the Sun.

Not Alone
The solar power station is faced by 63 small, flat mirrors. They reflect extra light onto the main mirror.

Whizzing in the Wind

Strong, steady winds can be put to work turning windmill blades. As the blades spin, they turn a shaft that generates electricity. These modern windmills come in several shapes. Groups of them are called wind farms.

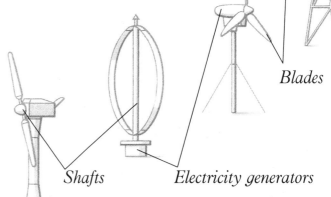

Blades

Shafts   *Electricity generators*

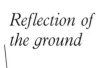

Reflection of the ground

A solar power station does not need a chimney – there are no fumes or ash!

This mirror is 42 metres wide. It is built onto the side of a building.

Water inside this tower turns to steam.

It can get as hot as 3,800°C inside this tower.

No Need for a Plug

Solar cells, made from slices of wafer-thin silicon, turn sunlight into electricity. This remote jungle telephone is powered by several solar cells.

Sunlight knocks electrons from the top layer to the bottom layer of silicon. This generates an electric current that is collected by the metal layers.

Sunlight
Metal
Silicon
Metal

ELECTRICITY

Electricity is used as a way of moving energy from place to place. It can take energy from burning coal in a power station into your home to work your television. Most electricity is generated in machines. Small machines, called dynamos, light the lights on bikes. Huge generators in power stations light whole cities. Pedal power works a dynamo, but steam produces the electricity in a power station. This steam is made by using the heat from burning fossil fuels or splitting atoms. Sunshine, falling water and whirling windmills can also generate electricity.

Dynamo

Mighty Machine
The big blue generator inside this power station is about ten times as tall as you!

This magnet spins round because it is fixed to a rod that touches the turning wheel.

Electricity is generated in this coil of wire by the spinning magnet.

Chimney

3. Steam surges from the boiler into the generator. It pushes round huge paddles, called turbines.

2. The burning coal makes water turn into steam.

1. Coal is crushed and then blown into the boiler to burn.

A pile of coal as heavy as 40 elephants is burnt each hour.

4. Turbines turn a massive magnet round 50 times a second.

5. The moving magnet creates an electric current in huge coils of wire.

First transformer

A condenser turns the hot steam into hot water.

Choice of Fuels
A power station uses just one sort of fuel to generate its electricity. This one burns coal, but other power stations use oil, natural gas or nuclear fuel.

Oil

Natural gas

Uranium

The cooling tower cools the hot water so that it can be used again.

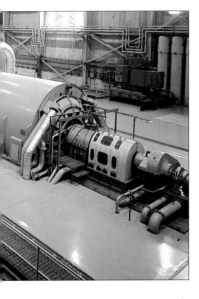

In Charge
Power stations can't be built near all the places that need electricity. So the electricity generated flows into a network of cables, called a grid. At the touch of a button, electricity is made to flow to wherever it is needed.

Electricity cables are laid under the ground in towns and cities.

Second transformer

Electricity is dangerous, so tall pylons hold the long cables high above the ground.

A substation makes electricity safe for you to use in your home.

Aluminium cable

Energy travels down the cables at about 250,000 kilometres a second – almost as fast as the speed of light!

Watt is Power?
The speed at which different machines use energy is measured in units called watts.

Electric clock (10 watts)

Going Up or Going Down?
Machines, called transformers, change the strength of an electric current. The current that flows between pylons has to be decreased to stop the cables from melting.

These children are pretending to be tiny parts of atoms, called electrons.

Each ball is a 'parcel' of electrical energy.

Pass the Parcel
People once thought that electricity flowed like water, which is why it was called a current. In fact, energy moves along a cable more like balls being passed down a line!

Vacuum cleaner (1,000 watts)

Welding machine (10,000 watts)

ENERGY FOR INDUSTRY

There are three main types of industries. Primary industries, such as farming, fishing and mining, take raw materials from the Earth. Manufacturing industries make, or manufacture, useful things from the raw materials. Service industries sell either these products, or skills such as cutting hair or mending a car. All industries need energy to work, so as the world becomes more industrialized, it needs more and more energy.

Industry is Born
In 1712, Thomas Newcomen invented a simple engine that could power many machines in a factory. By 1800, many people had left their farms to find factory jobs.

The steps of industry have to be taken one at a time – a jumper does not grow on a sheep, it has to be made!

Wool is manufactured from a fleece.

Muscle Power
In some parts of the world, animals still provide power. These cows are helping to make bricks by pulling clay up from the ground.

The Steps of Industry
All three types of industries are needed to produce most of the things that are sold in shops.

Fleece

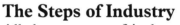
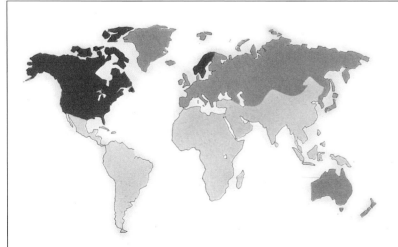

Energetic Industry
The darker areas on this map use more energy per person than the lighter ones. Much of this difference is due to the amount of industry a country has.

Growing wheat is a primary industry.

Getting raw materials from the Earth takes energy. The diggers that dug up this iron ore needed fuel.

Pass It On

Factories make masses of things quickly because workers are put in production lines. Rather than each person making a whole car, for example, each worker repeats a task, and then passes the unfinished car down the line.

The textile industry was the first industry to move its workers into machine-filled factories.

Three hundred years ago spinners worked in their own homes. There were no factories.

Grinding flour and baking bread are manufacturing industries.

Selling bread in a shop is a service industry.

If nobody buys the final product, all the time, money and energy spent making it are wasted.

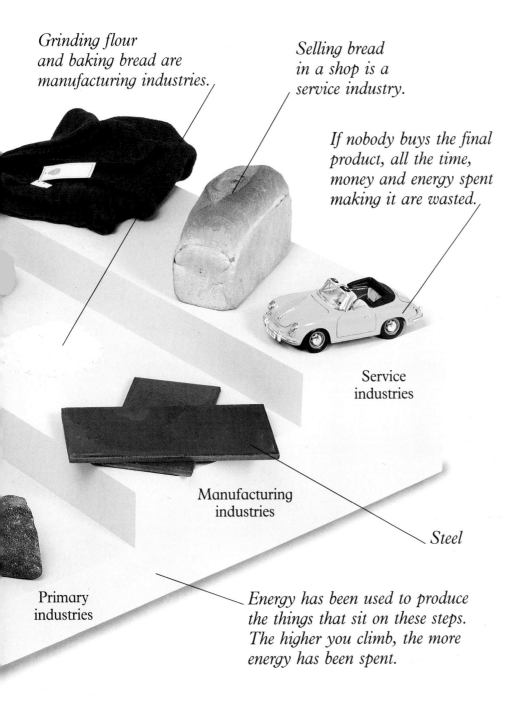

Service industries

Manufacturing industries

Steel

Primary industries

Energy has been used to produce the things that sit on these steps. The higher you climb, the more energy has been spent.

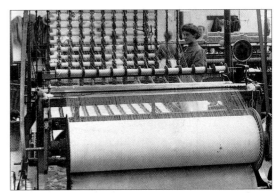

The noisy machines in the first factories were powered by water wheels and needed many workers.

Modern spinning machines run on electricity. Many of the workers have been replaced by computers!

RICHES OF THE EARTH

If the world was an apple, its crust would only be as thick as the peel. Yet this thin outer layer provides people with most of the ingredients, or raw materials, needed by industry to make things. For example, pencils are made from graphite, which is dug from the crust, and trees, which grow on it. The riches in this giant raw-material store are starting to run out, so some materials are now recycled. People are also looking for new supplies – one day lumps of metal may be vacuumed off the ocean floor!

Look Out Below
Photographs from satellites can be colour-coded to show where people should dig to find useful rocks. Silicon and salt will be found in the pale blue patches on this picture of Nevada in the USA. The black 'hole' is a lake!

Crater in the Crust
Rocks are scooped out of a huge hole, called a quarry, and taken away to build roads.

On the Surface
The plants that grow in the rich soil that covers the Earth's crust provide food.

Trees are cut down and turned into timber for tables and chairs.

Big Dig

Aluminium is made from a red rock called bauxite, which is stripped from the Earth's crust. About 2 kg are needed to make one aluminium pan. A mine in Weipa, Australia, has enough rock to make more than 1,000,000,000,000 aluminium pans!

Where on Earth?

Many of the everyday things in your home come from surprising places.

This rubber was produced by a tree.

Pottery comes from soft rock called clay.

Rocks are crushed to make a white powder called talc.

Leather is made from animal skin.

Out of Thin Air

Useful things are taken out of the air you breathe, as well as the ground you walk on. Liquid nitrogen is frozen out of air and then sprayed onto foods to freeze in their taste and goodness.

The crust is about six kilometres thick under the oceans, but it can be ten times thicker under land.

Trawlers take fish from the sea for you to eat.

Sand and gravel are scraped from the seabed and used by the building industry.

See the Salt

Hot sea water can be boiled away to leave behind salt crystals. You sprinkle these white grains on your dinner, but they are also put in glue and bubble bath!

THE FOOD INDUSTRY

Today, most people do not grow all their own food. Instead, farmers grow food and sell it to shops or, more often, to factories. A whole industry has grown up to bottle, can or freeze food so that it is tasty and safe to eat. It will also look good when it reaches your table many months later. Preserving chemicals may be injected into meat, and colouring from carrots is poured into bottled orange juice. Peas are frozen so fast that they are fresher than those sold by greengrocer's!

In the Can
Uncooked food is put in a can and boiled. When the food is cooked, the lid is quickly put on. The sealed can is then reheated to kill food-spoiling 'bugs'.

Peas are ruined if large ice crystals grow inside them, so they are frozen quickly.

Peas must be frozen within three hours of being picked, otherwise they lose their sweet taste and bright green colour.

The peas travel on a conveyor belt to be frozen. They have already been washed, and then boiled for two minutes.

Popping Pods
Big machines start to harvest peas as soon as they are sweet enough to be frozen. The peas are popped from their pods and sent straight to the factory.
The pods are left to fertilize the field.

Older peas are tougher, so they are sorted out and canned.

Pea Dance
As they are frozen by blasts of very cold air, the peas dance up and down. If the peas did not keep moving they would stick together.

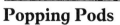

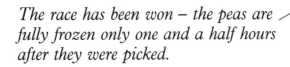

The race has been won – the peas are fully frozen only one and a half hours after they were picked.

Frozen food cannot spoil because it is too cold for germs, moulds and other food 'bugs' to grow.

Frozen In Time
Thawed two-year-old peas can taste as good as new if they have been stored in a place that is colder than -23°C.

Always Apricots
Apricots, like many foods, can be processed in different ways to make them last longer.

Over the Counter
When there are about 300 frozen peas in this scoop, it tips over and drops them into a plastic bag.

Dried apricots

Big Brew
Coffee beans are sent to computer-controlled factories to be cleaned and roasted. When they are roasted, coffee beans double in size, turn brown and start to smell like coffee. These beans can then be sold as they are or frozen and dried to make instant coffee.

Bottled apricots

Freshly roasted coffee beans

Coffee is one of about 600 foods that can be freeze-dried without losing their flavour.

Apricot jam

THE BREAD BUSINESS

Wheat

Bread of different kinds is eaten all over the world. Much of it is made from wheat, but millet cakes are popular in Africa and corn bread in America. Some people still bake their own bread, but most is made in factories and sold in shops. Many people work in this huge industry. Farmers grow grain, millers grind flour and bakers bake bread. But the bread business also employs drivers, dockers, accountants, engineers and even scientists, who breed better sorts of wheat.

No Knead
In just six minutes, this speedy mixer whisks the ingredients into a sticky dough. This batch will make 380 loaves.

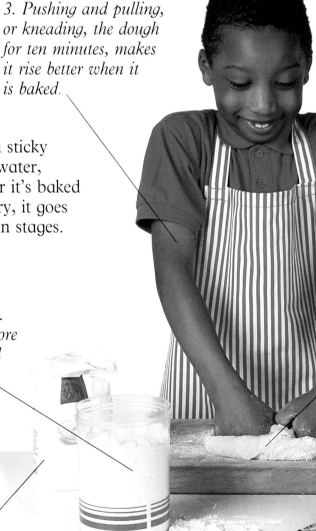

3. Pushing and pulling, or kneading, the dough for ten minutes, makes it rise better when it is baked.

All Mixed Up
Bread is made from a sticky mixture of flour and water, called dough. Whether it's baked at home or in a factory, it goes through the same main stages.

2. Flour is added to the sugar and yeast mixture. With a little salt and more water, this can be mixed to make a soft dough.

1. Sugar is mixed with yeast and water. Together they make gas bubbles, which will spread through the dough to make it rise.

Yeast

Grown to Grind
Truckloads of grain are sent to mills, crushed into flour and then made into bread.

Imports In

A doughnut factory in France may use local eggs, water, milk, yeast and margarine. But other ingredients have to be brought in, or imported, from all over the world.

Salt from China

Flour from the USA

Sugar from India

Cocoa from Brazil

Vegetable oil from Nigeria

Rising to the Occasion

This bread has just spent 54 minutes in a 'rising room', called a prover. It swells even more when it is baked.

4. Your dough now needs to rise. Cover it with a cloth and leave it for one hour in a warm place. In a factory, it is put into a prover.

One-Track Tins

Special suction cups suck the bread out of the tins. The baking tins then trundle down a conveyor belt to be rinsed and reused.

5. Your home-made bread is baked in a normal oven. Factory-made bread is cooked in one that is nearly as big as a tennis court!

Salt will stop puffed-up bread from collapsing.

This loaf needs about half a litre of water. A factory's bread batch needs about 200 times this amount!

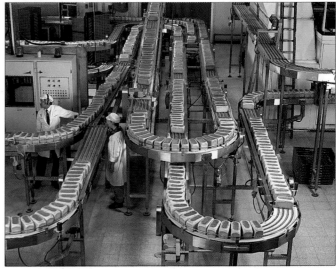

It may take you two hours and a lot of mixing to make just one loaf. A factory can bake 140 loaves a minute!

Cool Queue

Every week, more than 1.3 million loaves cool down as they wind around this twisting track on their way to be bagged.

WOOD

See the Saw
Inside a sawmill a big circular saw whizzes round and chops tree trunks into shorter pieces. These are then sent to a timber mill to be planked.

Every year huge numbers of trees are chopped down. If they were all piled together, they would make a block of wood seven kilometres high and one kilometre on each side. Half of this wood pile is burnt, because it is the only fuel that people in many countries can afford. One-third is cut up in timber mills and made into useful things, such as building beams or guitars. The rest of this valuable crop is made into paper for books like this one!

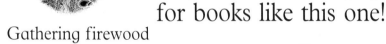

Gathering firewood

A Douglas fir tree can grow to be 40 times taller than you in just 30 years.

Wood can be burnt to make charcoal for barbecues!

About 12,000 sheets of paper, each the size of a page in this book, can be made from an average-sized fir tree.

Tree Peel
Every ten years people strip the bark from cork oak trees. After it has dried out, it is made into cork mats and stoppers for bottles. Only the outer bark is taken off; the young bark is left to protect the tree and to grow a new cork crop.

Branch Out
This enormous machine picks up whole, heavy trees and rips off all their bark and branches.

Chemicals in the bark are used to make ink.

Cutting wood into planks allows its grain, or pattern of fibres, to be seen.

Big branches, as well as tree trunks, are cut up into planks.

Planks have to be dried out, or seasoned, before they can be used.

Paper Maker

Inside a paper mill, washed and dyed wood pulp is poured onto a huge wire conveyor belt. Water drips out of the pulp to leave a wet sludge of paper fibres. These are squashed and dried to produce card for boxes or paper for books and tissues.

Woodwork

Not all wood is the same, so carpenters choose the woods they work with carefully.

Ash spade handles are hard to break.

Oak benches will not rot in the rain.

Spruce window frames are cheap and easy to make.

Planking Place

Tree trunks are sliced into thin planks in a timber mill. The long pieces of flat wood are sold and used to make floorboards, furniture and boats.

Worldwide, trees are being cut down seven times faster than they are being planted.

Board of Chips!

Chopped-up twigs are sprayed with glue and pressed flat to make chipboard. This is often used to make cheap furniture.

Twigs are made into chipboard.

No wood is wasted. Sawdust is used as a fuel in the ovens that dry out wet wood.

Break It Up

Factories, called pulp mills, break up whole fir, pine or spruce trees into pieces the size of grains of salt. This wood pulp is used to make paper.

METALS

Metals are found in the ground, hidden in special rocks, called ores. Tin, copper and iron all have to be taken out of their ores before a factory can melt and shape them into a can, pan or car. Pure metals, however, are usually too weak to be used in industry and have to be mixed together to make better metals called alloys. Lead is soft and tin breaks easily. Together they can make a strong tough alloy known as pewter.

Iron ore

Copper pan

Not Natural
Brass is an alloy, which means it can't be dug out of the ground. It is made by mixing two weaker metals, copper and zinc.

Brass is stronger than zinc or copper.

Zinc-coated bucket and wire

Precious Metals
Gold and silver are used to make far more than just jewellery. Gold is sprayed onto an astronaut's visor to reflect sunlight. Silver mixtures are used to make photographic films as they are sensitive to light.

Steel from Iron
Iron has a lot of carbon in it, which makes it crack easily. If some carbon is removed, iron turns into super-strong steel. This change starts in a blast furnace.

Limestone

Coke

Crushed iron ore

Blast furnace

Coke, limestone and iron ore heat up and turn into iron and a waste material called slag.

Hot air

Slag

Iron

1. Blasted Iron Ore
A stream of iron is flowing from this huge oven, called a blast furnace. It has been burned out of iron ore by blasts of hot air.

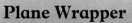

Big Dipper
Steel girders are dipped in a bath of melted zinc to stop them from going rusty. This process is known as galvanizing.

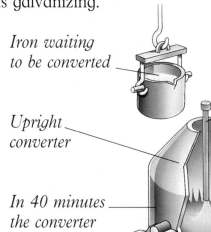

Plane Wrapper
Aluminium is a marvellous metal. Thin sheets are wrapped around chocolate to preserve its taste. Thick sheets are made into jumbo jets. Aluminium is used to make planes because it does not rust and it is very light. The aluminium is made as stiff as steel by adding a little copper.

Iron waiting to be converted

Upright converter

In 40 minutes the converter can make 350 tonnes of steel.

Oxygen rushes down this tube.

Scrap iron can be put into the converter too.

Rust Buster
You would not want to eat with rusty cutlery! So chromium is added to steel to make an alloy called stainless steel.

Tipped-up converter

When the strips of steel are cold they can be squashed by rollers into flat slabs.

Hot steel

2. Iron In, Steel Out
The liquid iron is poured into a converter. After a powerful jet of oxygen has burnt out the impurities and most of the carbon, the converter is tipped up to pour out steel.

3. Taking Shape
Hot, freshly made steel is poured into a big tray. When it has almost set, nozzles are opened and steel oozes out, like toothpaste out of a tube.

GLASS

Many things in your home, such as windows and light bulbs, are made of glass. This useful material is easy to shape and its three ingredients – sand, limestone and soda ash – are all common. When they are mixed and melted they form a sticky syrup which can be pulled, stretched or pressed. Most glass is breakable, but if hot glass is blasted with cold air it toughens up and can be used to make car windscreens. Glass with layers of plastic set in it can be strong enough to stop a speeding bullet!

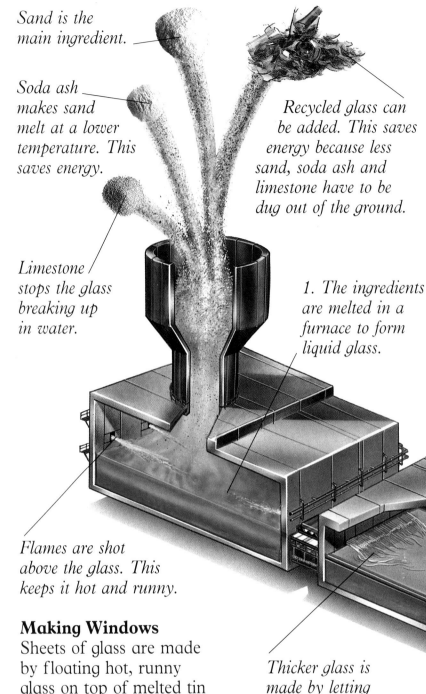

Sand is the main ingredient.

Soda ash makes sand melt at a lower temperature. This saves energy.

Limestone stops the glass breaking up in water.

Recycled glass can be added. This saves energy because less sand, soda ash and limestone have to be dug out of the ground.

1. The ingredients are melted in a furnace to form liquid glass.

Flames are shot above the glass. This keeps it hot and runny.

Thicker glass is made by letting more liquid glass pour into the tank.

Making Windows
Sheets of glass are made by floating hot, runny glass on top of melted tin in a huge tank. The glass spreads out on the tin to form a perfectly flat sheet.

Glass Carpet
If hot, runny glass is forced through tiny holes it turns into glass fibres. These threads are chopped up and pressed into thick mats. When unrolled, this prickly carpet helps to keep a building cool in summer and warm in winter.

Call for Glass
Phone calls used to travel down copper cables but these are now being replaced by long glass hairs, which are cheaper and lighter. Sounds are changed into light signals which are fired by lasers down the glass.

Blowing Bottles

Bottles are made by dropping hot glass into a mould and blowing it into shape.

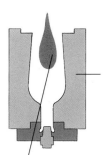

Mould

Blob of hot glass

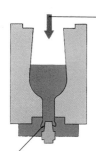

Air pushes the glass down.

The neck is formed.

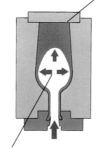

The top of the mould is put on.

Air pushes out the hot glass.

Cooling Time

Newly blown bottles are carried by a conveyor belt through a long tunnel, called a lehr, to cool down.

---

2. The glass floats on the tin. As is flows through the tank, the glass cools and begins to set.

3. Sticky, toffee-like glass leaves the huge tank and moves into a second, cooler oven.

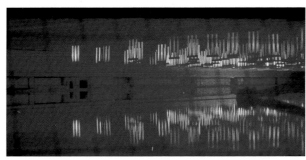

Too Hot to Handle

As the red-hot ribbon of runny glass cools, its surface settles into a flat layer and its base becomes as smooth as the tin 'lake' below.

4. Glass goes into another oven to be reheated, but not melted. It is allowed to cool slowly to stop it cracking.

Secret Ingredients

Cobalt turns glass bright blue.

Borax makes glass heat-proof.

Silver makes sunglasses darken in sunshine.

The glass is solid enough not to be dented by rollers.

Robot

The glass is about three metres wide.

Flat Out

The sheets of glass that roll out of the float glass machine are ready to be cut up into window panes.

A tiny diamond slices through the glass.

MAKING A CAR

Model T

Every few seconds, somewhere in the world, a brand-new car rolls off a production line and out of a car factory. Each car is made from raw materials, such as iron ore, sulphur and sand, which have been shaped into more than 30,000 parts! Most of this 'jigsaw puzzle' is put together on a kind of giant conveyor belt. Each area of the factory puts on a few particular pieces, for example, the body shop adds the roof, but never the seats. The first car made like this was the Model T Ford.

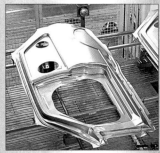

Stamp It Out
Sheets of cold steel are stamped into shape by machines called presses. A press room can be the size of three football stadiums!

Each car body is made from more than 20 pieces, or panels, of steel.

Press

Steel

The start of the 'conveyor belt'.

About 80 per cent of a car is made of iron and steel.

Start with Steel
Steel is the most important ingredient for making cars. Rolling mills press hot steel into thin sheets. These are then rolled up and sent to car factories.

A roller test is used to check that the car is working.

Apart from their colour, all the cars made on this production line are the same.

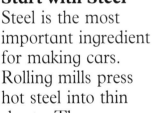

Cars are washed and polished before they leave the factory to be sold.

Ready to Go
Cars were only invented about 100 years ago but there are now more than 400 million of them.

Built to Bounce
To make your journey smooth, tyres are made of rubber and filled with air.

Strands of steel or nylon toughen the tyres.

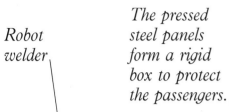

Robot welder

The pressed steel panels form a rigid box to protect the passengers.

Robots in Charge

The steel sides, roof and doors have to be joined together. This is done by welding – making the metal melt and stick together. Using more than 1,000 welds, robots can build a car body in just 42 seconds.

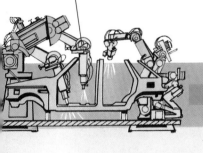

Heavy cars use more fuel. So more and more metal parts, such as bumpers, are being made of plastic.

Robot painter

Mechanical Monets

Cars are painted by robots with sprays. The robots are not harmed by paint fumes and can put paint on quickly and accurately.

The doors are removed so that the inside can be reached more easily.

The car is lowered onto an engine, which was built on a separate production line. This may have been in another country!

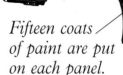

Bare steel base

Top coat

Fifteen coats of paint are put on each panel.

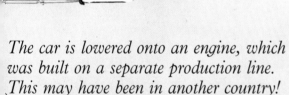

Robots add windows.

Each worker repeats the same job over and over again.

Pile Up

A new car may not be as new as you think. Up to 40 per cent of the steel may have come from old cars! Recycling scrap steel saves raw materials and energy.

Together at Last

The engine is the heart of the car but it is not added to the body until near the end of the production line.

CHEMICAL INDUSTRIES

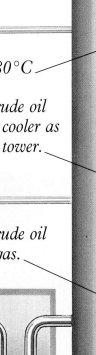

Oil refinery

Soap, fertilizer and glue are just a few of the useful products of the chemical industries. They are made by combining different substances. Crude oil is the main raw material for these industries. The carbon and hydrogen in oil can be made to join up in different ways to make more than half a million things, such as petrol, paint or pills! This manufacturing starts in special factories called refineries.

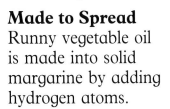

Made to Spread
Runny vegetable oil is made into solid margarine by adding hydrogen atoms.

Split It Up!
Crude oil is split into useful oils inside a distillation tower at a refinery. The oils are separated by being boiled into a gas and then cooled back into a liquid.

Distillation tower

110°C

Cooling oil drips from the edge of this 'saucer' into the tray below.

Kerosene is the fuel used by aeroplanes.

180°C

The cloud of crude oil gets cooler and cooler as it wafts up the tower.

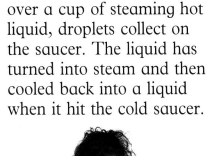

Liquid Again
If you put a saucer over a cup of steaming hot liquid, droplets collect on the saucer. The liquid has turned into steam and then cooled back into a liquid when it hit the cold saucer.

Lubricating oil makes machines run smoothly.

At 385°C, crude oil turns into a gas.

Crude oil is pumped into a furnace to be boiled into a gas.

Very hot liquid turns into a gas.

Gas cools into a liquid.

All Change

Chlorine keeps the water in swimming pools clean and safe to swim in. It is made in a factory by passing electricity through salty water. The electric current makes the atoms in the salt and water rearrange and produce chlorine.

Cat Cracker

Oil is made up of long chains of carbon and hydrogen atoms. Useful chemicals, called petrochemicals, are made by breaking up these chains. This is done by heating the oil in tanks called cat crackers. The small chains can be used to make useful things such as shampoo.

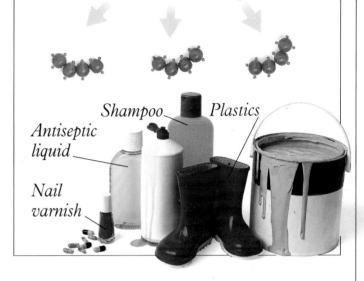

Carbon atom

Hydrogen atom

Hydrogen atoms are forced between the carbon atoms to break up the chain.

Antiseptic liquid

Shampoo

Plastics

Nail varnish

The gases that come out of the top of the tower are made into plastics.

One-fifth of each barrel of crude oil separates into petrol.

Petrol is the most common fuel used to power cars.

When the cloud of crude oil reaches this height, it is cool enough for diesel to turn into a liquid.

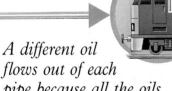

Diesel is the fuel used by many trains.

A different oil flows out of each pipe because all the oils in crude oil cool into liquids at different temperatures.

Dark industrial oil is burnt in factories and power stations.

Bitumen is the first oil to flow out of the tower.

Thick, sticky bitumen is spread on the surface of roads.

Sulphur So Good

About 150 million tonnes of sulphuric acid are used every year to help make things such as fertilizer, paper and explosives! This acid is made by heating a yellow rock called sulphur.

PLASTICS

Plastics are amazing materials. They don't rot like wood or rust like some metals, and they are light and easy to shape. Plastic pens, shoes and even surfboards are all made from oil or coal. Chemicals are taken from these fossil fuels and turned into small, white pellets. These are then melted and blown to form bags or rolled flat to make floor tiles. Buckets, bowls and boxes are usually shaped by being injected into moulding machines.

Get Set or Go?
Some plastics, such as Bakelite, are like bread! Once they have been 'baked' they cannot be reheated and made into new shapes. A melamine mug will not change shape when hot drinks are poured into it. Polystyrene and polythene are more like chocolate – they can be melted again and again. Each time the mixture cools, it sets into the shape of the mould it has been poured into.

The two halves of the steel mould lock tightly together.

Bowled Out

Washing-up bowls are made by injecting melted plastic pellets into the space between two halves of a steel mould. The plastic cools inside the mould and sets into a bowl shape.

Cold water cools down the plastic after it has been moulded.

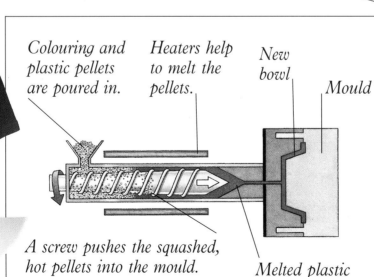

Colouring and plastic pellets are poured in.

Heaters help to melt the pellets.

New bowl

Mould

A screw pushes the squashed, hot pellets into the mould.

Melted plastic

Each bowl needs this amount of colouring.

Two handfuls of polypropylene plastic pellets make each bowl.

Temperatures of 280°C are needed to melt the pellets and make them flow into this mould.

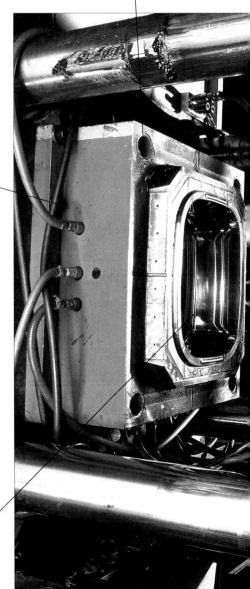

Don't Throw It Away

You are wasting energy when you throw away plastic bottles or bags. Most plastic 'rubbish' can be turned into new things, such as the filling for sleeping bags, or fuel bricks which can burn better than coal!

Plastic Products

Nose cone

A plane's nose cone is made from glass-reinforced plastic, not metal, so that radar waves can pass through it.

Polystyrene is plastic too.

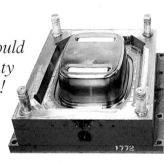

Each half of this bowl mould weighs as much as twenty eight-year-old children!

Many electronic gadgets, such as personal stereos, are made of a tough plastic called ABS.

This half of the mould moves back to let the warm, newly shaped bowl drop onto a conveyor belt.

Four bowls can be made in a minute.

Food slides off the slippery plastic, known as Teflon, used to coat the surface of nonstick pans.

Under the rim, you may see a line. This is where the two halves of the mould met.

Jets of air blow the bowl off the mould when it is finished.

Every bowl that comes out of this machine is exactly the same shape.

Plastic packaging keeps food fresh for longer. For example, polythene bags stop bread from drying out.

TEXTILES

Most of the things you wear are textiles, and so are carpets and tents. A textile is anything that is made of threads. Wool comes from animals, cotton from plants, but many threads are synthetic – they are made in a factory. Most natural threads, or fibres, have to be twisted together, or spun, to make longer threads. Synthetic fibres can be woven into textiles without spinning. Fibres are chosen for their best qualities: wool makes warm jumpers but is far too heavy to be used for parachutes!

'Paper' Money
Banknote paper is made from cotton rags because ordinary paper is too weak.

These shiny silk threads were spun by a caterpillar but woven by a machine.

Velvet is a bit like a carpet. The threads on its surface are trimmed to make a textile with 'bristles'.

A rayon blouse is woven from threads made out of wood! Rayon looks like silk but is cheaper, stronger and does not crease.

Leggings do not get baggy knees if they are made from synthetic Lycra. This textile bounces back into shape.

Polyester socks

Rainbow Factory!
Clothes would be very dull if they were all off-white, so fibres are usually dyed. Fibres or woven materials are put in tanks of coloured water and left until every thread has soaked up the dye and changed colour.

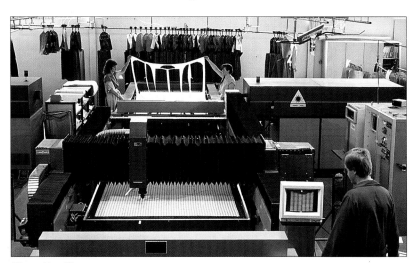

Cut It Out
Computer-controlled lasers cut cloth into shapes that can be sewn up into clothes. The beam of light slices through hundreds of layers of cloth at once.

Wool keeps you warm because air gets trapped inside its soft, springy threads.

Natural cotton threads feel soft. Synthetic polyester threads are tough. When they are twisted together they make a soft, tough T-shirt.

Hot Shower
Melted plastic is pumped through a set of holes in a spinneret to form a shower of nylon strands. When these fibres are cool and hard they can be knitted into stockings, wound into ropes or woven into fabric.

Nylon rope can be stronger than steel!

Nylon threads are woven into a strong rucksack.

This jacket is made from oil! Its nylon and Pertex® fibres mix to make a textile that keeps out the rain and stops you getting too hot.

Plastic Knitting
A nylon stocking is made from just one long thread of nylon. The thread is three kilometres long and has to be looped around itself more than one million times.

A nylon stocking is stretchy.

White fibres from cotton plants have been dyed blue and woven into tough denim material since 1874.

Your feet will not get wet in these textile shoes because they are woven with waterproof fibres.

Well Suited
Top-class skiers wear skintight suits made of Gore-Tex®. This synthetic material keeps them completely dry without making them too hot.

Oven Ready?
This suit is so shiny that it reflects heat, like light bouncing back from a mirror! It is made by coating materials, such as wool or rayon, with aluminium foil.

BUILDING

Sears Tower

The invention of new materials and new ways of building has enabled cities to shoot up into the sky. Skyscrapers are not held up by wood, brick or stone walls but by strong steel skeletons on which walls and windows are simply hung like curtains. Today's tallest office building, the Sears Tower in Chicago, USA, has 110 floors but engineers now think they could build towers that are six times taller. Imagine taking a lift to the 660th floor!

Concrete Creation
Many modern buildings, such as the Sydney Opera House, are made of concrete. This artificial rock is made by roasting clay and limestone to make cement, and then adding sand and water. Stretched steel cables inside the concrete stop it cracking.

Clay

Limestone   Sand   Water

Architects designed this skyscraper so that the steel supporting frame is on the outside.

Flexible glue makes sure that the windows don't pop out when the building sways in the wind!

Helicopter pad

47th floor

All large parts, such as wall panels, were brought in by trucks at night. This was the only time that the streets of Hong Kong were empty enough!

Steel was sprayed to stop it rusting.

Eight steel columns are buried more than 30 metres into solid rock to support the bank.

Growing Up
Building started on the headquarters of the Hong Kong and Shanghai Bank in 1981. It was finished in 1985.

This picture of the bank was taken in February 1984. Steel is being positioned on the 28th floor.

Each of the six red cranes could lift steel as heavy as ten elephants!

The workers clambered about the building on scaffolding made of bamboo.

About 3,500 tonnes of aluminium were used to make the wall panels.

On some days there were more than 4,500 builders, electricians, painters and plumbers working on the bank.

Telephone wires, computer links and electric cables are hidden under the aluminium floor panels.

Fireproof foil wrapping

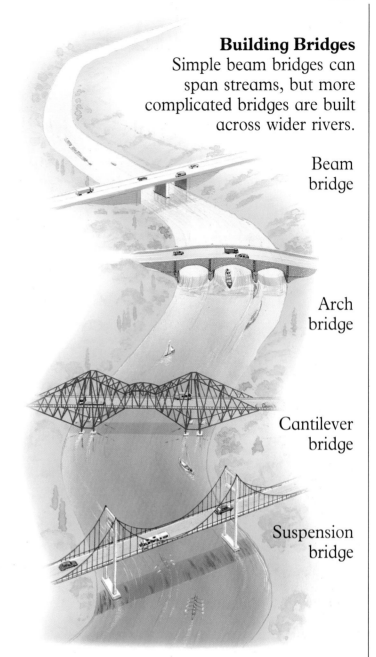

Building Bridges
Simple beam bridges can span streams, but more complicated bridges are built across wider rivers.

Beam bridge

Arch bridge

Cantilever bridge

Suspension bridge

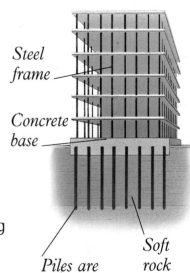

Rock Steady
Buildings need a strong base, or foundation, to stop them sinking, slipping sideways or being blown over by the wind. Tall buildings are held down by long steel or cement piles.

Steel frame

Concrete base

Piles are pushed into solid rock.

Soft rock

HIGH-TECH INDUSTRIES

Robotic Retriever
Robots work in many industries. This one is whizzing between tall shelves to select and collect computer parts.

Silicon crystal

Scientists' newest ideas are used by high-tech industries to make amazing electronic gadgets or marvellous medicines. Microchips are perhaps the best of these brilliant ideas. These electronic circuits are the 'brains' that control computers, fly planes or open shop doors. They are made by growing melted sand into shiny silicon crystals that are as long as your arm. Slices are cut off the crystals, and tiny chips are etched on the slices. Each chip is small enough to fit on the tip of your finger but is as complicated as a jumbo jet!

Cooking Chips
Slices of silicon are baked in a hot oven that contains special gases to create the complicated chip patterns.

A chip can work very, very fast because information does not have far to travel between its thousands of tiny parts.

This chip is new. The first one was made in 1958.

Each chip is put in a plastic or pottery case to keep it clean.

Circular wafers of silicon are diced up into hundreds of small, square chips.

There are 236 chips on this slice.

Electricity flows through the microscopic lines, layers and islands on the surface of the chip.

Making Medicine

Many modern drugs are manufactured in laboratories. This skilled worker, known as a technician, is making a type of medicine called an antibody. Eventually it will be given to people as an injection to prevent them catching deadly diseases.

Whatever Next?

These inventions seem amazing today, but in the next century many people may own them.

Videophones for voices with pictures

Carbon fibre is twice as strong as steel.

This light tennis racket still will not break when you smash a ball.

Materially Different

New, better materials are being invented all the time. This high-tech racket is lighter and stronger because it is made from a special mixture of carbon and plastic.

Metal pins fix the chip into a circuit board.

Electronic instructions flow between copper tracks on the plastic circuit board.

This calculator is controlled by just one chip.

Think First

Many years of research are carried out by scientists before high-tech products, such as video laserdisks, are manufactured and sold.

Computers that listen and talk

Electric cars for city driving

Some chips can add up more than 25 million sums a second!

SERVING YOU

When you think of the word 'industry' you probably think of a noisy factory that makes things such as cars. But an industry is any sort of work that creates wealth. Many businesses do not produce anything. Instead, they make sure that items manufactured in factories are transported, stored, insured and sold. Shops, banks, hairdressers, taxis and hotels all provide a service in exchange for money – they are known as service industries.

Keeping Shop
In many countries, most things are sold from outdoor markets, not brightly lit shops.

A shirt is sold, not made, in a shop. So a shop is part of a service industry.

In shops you have to choose between different makes, or brands, of the same thing. The companies that make them must compete for your money!

To speed up your shopping, most things are now weighed and put in packets before they reach the shop.

Money on the Move
The money you put, or deposit, in a bank does not stay locked in a safe. The banking industry lends it to companies who need money, either to build new factories or to buy modern machinery.

Funny Money
The leisure industry is growing because people have more time and money to spend on having fun in theme parks, theatres, cinemas and sports centres.

In Store For You

You don't go to a leather factory to buy a football. It is much easier to visit a toy shop or perhaps a large store that sells everything from telescopes to raspberries!

Bright pictures on the box tempt you to buy this telescope.

Laser pens at the checkout pass the information on bar codes to a computer. When enough items have been sold, the computer orders some more.

Bananas can be brought in, or imported, from abroad. Many things are transported long distances before you buy them.

Shopkeepers like to make it easy for you to spend money, so they provide trolleys.

The shop charges you more for this ball than they paid for it. Some of the difference in price pays for the running of the shop. The rest is profit.

Buy Me!

It is no good producing wonderful things if nobody knows they exist. The advertising industry lets people know what is for sale. One way of doing this, is to put up neon signs.

Accidents Do Happen

Trucks can crash, factories may burn down and homes are sometimes flooded. This is why people insure their property. When things go wrong, the insurance industry pays to put them right.

At Your Service

Life would be very different without the skills of the people, such as doctors, who are part of a service industry.

Telephone engineers

Postal workers

Police officers

Doctors and nurses

Teachers

GLOSSARY

Alloy A mixture of two or more metals.

Atom A tiny particle that consists of a nucleus, containing protons and neutrons, surrounded by a cloud of electrons. Everything is made from atoms.

Baker A person who earns money by baking bread and cakes.

Barrel A large container. Oil is measured in barrels holding 159 litres each.

Chemical A material made entirely of atoms joined together in the same way.

Coal dust Dust produced when coal is dug. It makes breathing hard for miners.

Coke A hard, black material made by heating coal. It is used to get iron from iron ore.

Crude oil Oil as it comes out of the ground before it has been refined.

Dynamo A device that uses a spinning magnet and coils of wire to change mechanical energy into electrical energy.

Electronic circuit A collection of electrical parts, including microchips, connected together to do something useful.

Factory A place where things are made for sale.

Fossil fuel Plant and animal remains from millions of years ago that can be burnt to release energy. Coal, oil and natural gas are fossil fuels.

Freeze-drying A way of preserving food by sucking the water out of it while it is frozen.

Impurity Anything that should not be present in a chemical or other material.

Laser A device that produces strong, pure light which can be used to cut things or to send messages.

Microchip A tiny piece of silicon that contains electronic switches. Computers are made from microchips.

Miller A person who works in a mill, grinding cereals, such as wheat, into flour.

Ore A rock that contains a useful amount of metal.

Peat Moist, rotted, squashed plants that would eventually turn into coal. Peat can be used as fuel.

Pneumatic drill A tool for breaking through hard materials. It is powered by air, which is squeezed into a small space and then released.

Power station A building where electrical power is generated. Power stations release energy from coal, oil, natural gas, uranium, falling water and even sunlight.

Raw material Anything, such as stone or oil, from which other useful materials or products are made.

Reactor Large container in which heat is produced from nuclear fuel.

Recycling Reusing something instead of throwing it away. Recycling glass, paper or steel saves raw materials and energy.

Robot A machine that works like a person but is controlled by a computer.

Rubber A sticky, stretchy material made from the juice of rubber trees. Synthetic rubber can be made from oil.

Rust A brown coating that forms on iron or steel when they come in contact with water and air.

Silicon A substance found in sand and some rocks. It conducts electricity slightly. Silicon is used to make microchips.

Synthetic Any material made by people to imitate something natural.

Uranium A heavy radioactive metal which is the main ingredient of nuclear fuel.

Well A deep hole drilled into the ground to reach water, oil or natural gas.

Acknowledgments

Photography: Andy Crawford, Steve Gorton, Kevin Mallett and Dave Rudkin.
Additional photography: Philip Dowell, Andreas von Einsiedel, Chas Hawson, David Johnson, Colin Keates, Gary Kevin, Dave King, Tim Ridley, Andrew McRobb, Stephen Shott, James Stevenson and Clive Streeter.
Illustrations: Peter Bull, Michael Fisher, Roy Flooks, Roger Goode, Tim Hayward, Aziz Khan, Pavel Kostal, Stewart Lafford, Jason Lewis, David More, Sue Oldfield, Alex Pang, Darren Pattenden, Sebastian Quigley, Clare Roberts, Craig Warwick, Mark Watkinson and Steve Weston.
Models: Donks Models.
Thanks to: Lois Carleton at Sir Norman Foster and Partners, London; The Colour Company; Dave Drayton, Chris Hicks and Sid Holborough at Addis Ltd. in Swansea; Emma Hughes at Texas Instruments, Bedford; David Jones of Jones Engineering, Birmingham; Bob Keay, Peter Lamb and Mr. Singh at British Bakeries, Forest Gate, London; Jenny Lewis at Imperial College, London; Norrie Carr Model Agency; Prince Racquets; Tony Reid; Laurie Ridgwell at Olympus Sport; Scallywags Child Model Agency; Jane Thomas; Julie Whittaker; Philip Wolfenden at British Steel.

INDEX